Peonies in Winter

Peonies in Winter

A Journey Through Loss, Grief, and Healing

Sally Rosenthal

Independently published

Editing, print layout, e-book conversion, and cover design by DLD Books Editing and Self-Publishing Services

DLD Books
www.dldbooks.com

Copyright 2021 by Sally H. Rosenthal
All rights reserved

Some of the material in this book was previously published in Magnets and Ladders, an online journal of Behind Our Eyes, and in a small quarterly called La Joie: The Journal Honoring All Creatures.

ISBN: 9798776767661

In Appreciation

All proceeds from the sale of this book will be donated to Guiding Eyes for the Blind in thanks for my three remarkable guide dogs: Boise, Greta, and Laurence. To learn more about this organization, see www.guidingeyes.org.

Dedication

In memory of my husband,
Sandy Rosenthal,
March 16, 1950–May 13, 2019

And to my cat, Tamsin, who shares the journey

Contents

In Appreciation 5
Dedication 7
Introduction 11

Across My Kitchen Table 13
Peonies in Winter 15
Kathleen in 1927 19
D–Day Vigil 21
Charles Palmer 23
Needs Must 25
Penny Candy 27
Feeding Spot 29
Reading with Corky 31
Solace 33
Mother's Day 35
A Daughter's Goodbye 37
Shadow 39
Farewell 41
My Hands 43
Letting Go and Holding On 45
The Gift 47
Oxygen 49
The Last Spring 51
Each Day a Blessing 53
Laurence's Promise 55
Beyond Bereft 57
Loss 59

Two Vigils 61
Running Free 63
Fragments of Poems 65
Hopeful Hands 67
The Chosen 69
Silent Night 71
Sitting in the Dark 73
Living with Intention 75
Here 77
Liminal Time 79
Night Visitor 81
Nine Months 83
Night Wind 85
Brittle with Age 87
Tamsin in Repose 89
A Matter of Perspective 91

Resources 93
Acknowledgments 95
About the Author 97

Introduction

Anyone who reads this book needs to know two things: I am a private person who did not write any of the poems and prose included here for a wide audience, and this is a book I wish I had not been in the position of writing.

Initially, I wrote most of this collection as a member of a small critique group that met monthly. I also gave a few poems to friends. That was as far as I was willing to go. While my colleagues were busy with publishing their work in journals and as books, I was content to hand a poem, literally or metaphorically, to another reader in the hope that she or he might find help, empathy, or solace. It was my idea of the literary equivalent of sitting at my kitchen table with that friend as we shared cups of coffee and whatever my work brought to the surface.

However, several friends urged me to compile a collection to reach more people. While the material included here is drawn from my own life and experiences, I began to realize that many individuals were also struggling with issues such as the deaths of spouses and parents, aging bodies, illness, caregiving, and mapping ways forward into unknown territory, either alone or in very changed circumstances.

While I wrote many of the poems as a way to unearth and process my reactions, it wasn't until I viewed them as a whole that I saw that the majority of the pieces were about dearly loved people and animals who had died. It also became apparent that all of them had made me the person who was able to provide care for a chronically ill husband. As I reread my words, I would have given almost anything to trade the words for another chance for more time with the people and animals I had lost. Sadly, life doesn't give any of us that option. So, I decided to keep their memories alive through words and to send those words wherever this book might take them.

I believe we all walk with some degree of sadness and bewilderment as we seek to live with loss. Although I have never believed in closure, I do think that, after loss and change, we are, at our core, resilient human beings who can come out of the shadow of sorrow and choose to take small steps at first and then larger ones into a future—one that is quite different but, nonetheless, beckoning.

Across My Kitchen Table

Shared only among friends for years,
my poems now travel to strangers.
Not without trepidation, I offer each one
as I would a cup of coffee to a guest,
hoping words will heal broken hearts
while we unravel our webs of grief.

Peonies in Winter

When I was in my still-invincible twenties, I sported a tote bag that proclaimed, "When the going gets tough, the tough go shopping." In my innocence, I had not yet experienced the losses that come with age. Yes, as an extremely premature baby, I had had a shaky start in life and a childhood spent in doctors' offices and hospitals, but these experiences made me believe that I really was invincible. After all, I had already paid my dues to random fate. I saw only the humor in the bag's slogan. I didn't realize that to be alive, at any age, is to be vulnerable and small in the face of chance.

Decades later, I have no idea what happened to that tote bag. Perhaps it vanished with the innocence of my twenties. Having become sadder and wiser with age, I no longer believe in my ability to outwit fate. Although I don't follow tote bag slogans these days, I do have a way of fooling myself, even for a few hours, that I inhabit an ordered universe—well, if not a universe, at least an ordered apartment. Nothing convinces me more that I can create order out of chaos than cleaning out closets.

That is how I found myself one snowy February morning, almost a year into the pandemic, standing in front of a cluttered bathroom storage closet.

The closet and its jumble were a metaphor for what my life had become during the previous year. My husband, following years of chronic illness, died suddenly from an unrelated brainstem aneurysm. A few months after Sandy's death, I moved to another apartment in my retirement community. Laurence, my third guide dog, decided it was time to hang up his harness and went to Florida to spend his retirement years with close friends of mine. Just when I thought things couldn't get much worse, a pandemic hit. It was definitely time for a closet overhaul.

As I tossed empty boxes, tissues, and other detritus into a trash bag, my hand fell upon a small box tucked into a corner. Opening the box, I realized, to my amazement, that it was a bottle of peony cologne, one of the flower essences I loved but could no longer wear. Sandy gave me rose, lavender, iris, and peony colognes on special occasions and holidays. When I moved, I thought I had donated whatever fragrances I had on hand to my church's flea market. Apparently not.

The sense of smell is so evocative. To catch even a whiff of the peony cologne was to find myself transported back to the occasion on which Sandy gave it to me. No widow wants to go there. In addition, peonies made me remember the peonies that bloomed, for only a few weeks, in late spring in my American grandparents' back yard when I was a little girl, happy and safe in a closely knit family.

On that February morning, I felt far from being loved and secure. I doubted I could stand to smell peonies, but with a tug of nostalgia mixed with pain, I sprayed a little on my wrist.

To my surprise, I smiled as I inhaled the scent. Of course there were tears in my eyes, too, but the overall emotion was one of bittersweet joy. I wasn't a melancholy, aging widow; I was someone who had been loved throughout her life. The scent of peonies turned a sad winter morning into a time when spring and love had graced my life.

It is my hope that anyone reading this book can, in whatever way is meaningful, find small joys amid sorrow. They are all around, quietly waiting to be noticed. Perhaps there will even be a hint of peonies in the air.

Kathleen in 1927

Coltishly long–legged with
fine hair lifted gently by a summer breeze,
my eleven–year–old mother sits, half–child and half–woman,
atop a split–rail fence on her grandparents' farm.
Glancing shyly up at the camera,
hands folded and with a half smile,
she leaves a sepia image of a
budding English rose not yet
come to full bloom in a long–ago Yorkshire meadow.

D–Day Vigil

On tenterhooks in her parents' home
in the war–ravaged English Midlands,
she sat and watched as the sky darkened
with fog and clusters of aircraft,
great birds of prey now bent on
an unknown mission of salvation,
forming a relentless migration toward the coast.

With restless energy, she stirred a pot of lentil soup,
switched on the wireless, and put the kettle on the hob.
Sensing her American paratrooper beau
was involved in this frenzy, the young woman
who would become my mother prayed silently
amid the sounds of droning aircraft and simmering soup.

Charles Palmer

I never met Charles Palmer. An ocean separated us. By the time I made my first trip to England in 1979, he had been dead for almost twenty years.

During that trip, I sat on a bench across the road from a house in the Midlands city of Leicester. A single home with a bright blue door and a well-tended garden, it was not unlike others on East Park Road.

Only the American tourist on the bench knew how special it was. Charles Palmer had lived there with his wife, Harriet, and their two daughters, Mabel and Kathleen, the latter of whom became my mother.

As a child in a small Pennsylvania town where Kathleen had settled with her American GI husband, I absorbed the stories my mother told of her home and family. While I could recount tales about my grandmother and aunt, I knew little about my grandfather.

This dearth of knowledge came not from lack of love on my mother's part but rather from the man himself. Born in 1880, Charles was too old for military service in both World Wars, but his age did not exclude him from serving on the home front as a nightly air raid warden. In the manner typical of many British men of his generation, he went about his rounds in the blackout and did what he could to keep his neighbors safe from German bombs.

When morning came, he went to his job as a wood turner, often stepping through the rubble remaining from destroyed homes and businesses. With dignity and quiet determination, he simply did what needed to be done.

Spending his days at work fashioning bowls, candlesticks, and other useful items of practical beauty from burnished wood, he set an example for the unborn granddaughter he would never hold in his arms.

I find it strangely miraculous that a man whose voice I have never heard or with whom I haven't shared a pot of tea could have played such a central role in my life. His "getting on with things" spirit found its way into my DNA, as did his working with wood. Not as creative with my hands as Charles was, I became a writer, whose words flowed out of her onto the wood pulp of paper, until blindness forced me to use a computer.

No, Charles Palmer and I never met, but if we had, I like to think he would have been as quietly proud of me as I have been of him. Although we inhabited different times and places, I believe we would have recognized each other as kindred souls.

Needs Must

Massive paws lumbering along
familiar English garden paths,
my aunt's gentle mastiffs are perplexed
to find roses replaced by rhubarb.
Where larkspur and lavender flourished,
courgettes and carrots await harvesting.
Near dark, gnarled yew trees from which
the ancient house takes its name,
rows of potatoes and peas are nourished
by soil and sun in a ravaged
and rationed nation's victory garden.
Nature's abundance will feed
the homefront until, Hitler defeated,
English roses bloom again.

Penny Candy

Snow crunching beneath our boots, Grandpa and I
trudge small-town streets on our daily ramble.
His measured, arthritic pace slows even more
to match my unsteady gait as
my braced legs struggle on frozen pavements.
With my mittened hand in his, I feel secure
and know he will not let me slide or fall.

He greets each person we pass and stops to talk
while we wait for our Boston Terrier, who must
read the neighborhood canine news on every tree trunk.

Reaching the fire station, we drop in to catch up
with Grandpa's cronies, one of whom lifts me high
so my four-year-old hands can touch the gleaming red engine.
At Beyer's Bakery, a warm cocoon of cinnamon and sugar
engulfs us as we choose vanilla twists to take home.

Our last destination takes the most time as
I carefully survey the penny candy counter in Schwartz's corner
    shop,
spending the coin Grandpa gives me on
malted milk balls, snowcaps, chocolate squares, taffy chunks,
    and red licorice.

Heading home, an old man, a cantankerous dog, and
a little girl stamp snow from their boots and paws
while her hand clutches a small brown bag filled with love.

Feeding Spot

Swathed in hand-knit scarves and a thick wool shawl,
I watch my breath rise in misty puffs
as the pale winter sun peeks above the horizon on
my great-aunt's hardscrabble Pennsylvania tobacco farm.
My five-year-old hands clutch a baby bottle
of warm milk as the doe sucks it dry before turning
to Aunt Ivy for the apple slices on offer.
Rescued as an orphan fawn and nursed to health
in a box of blankets beside a wood-burning stove
in the old farmhouse's kitchen, Spot was released
to the wilderness, only to return
each morning for her treats as her mate, a buck
with, to my child's eyes, an enormous rack of antlers that surely
    reached the clouds,
waited from afar on the frozen ground of a neighboring field.
With adult hindsight, I realize we did Spot no favor
by teaching her to trust humans in a poor county
where venison on the table helped families
make it through the lean months of unforgiving winters.
Still, sixty years on, I hope Spot and her mate
escaped the hunters' arrows and buckshot and that their
    generations to come
survived to nibble the green sweetness of next year's spring.

Reading with Corky

Bathed in memory's golden glow,
a sixty-year-old image makes me smile:

A shy, small girl carrying homemade cookies
and a tattered copy of Beautiful Joe
settles on the top step leading to a back porch.
Despite October's chill and the coming dusk,
she savors these hours between school and supper
when she can claim this time and space as her own.

Pressing close in hope of a cookie,
her Boston Terrier gets his wish.
Marshall Saunders' much-loved novel
of a dog's triumph over abuse
has made the girl vow to always love animals
as much as books.
As shrieks of neighborhood children
playing football fall away,
she draws Corky nearer
and loses herself in printed words of kindness.

Solace

In memory of Kathleen Bennett, 1916–2008

I brought my mother a dog to polish
the dullness of a nursing home routine
and make it sparkle with Labrador enthusiasm.

I brought my mother a dog to remind her
she was the same person whose ninety-one years
had been blessed by canine devotion.

I brought my mother a dog to salve
my conscience for the care I could not provide
and to assuage my guilt for the luxuries I had at home
of meals of my own choosing, hot cups of tea, and quiet privacy.

I brought my mother a dog a few hours
before she died. As I held her waif-like hand,
listening to her changing breath and bidding her safe travel,
I prayed that the woman in the nursing home bed
that held no hint of home realized
I had brought us both a dog.

Mother's Day

On the second Mother's Day without her,
my mother's daughter woke to the
ache of memory and warmed arthritic hands
on a cup of coffee while sitting with
the yellow Labrador who had loved them both.

Slipping a body grown lean through loss
into slim black jeans and topping them with
a pink sweater reminiscent of English roses
tended by the war–bride mother in a small-town American
      garden and

not giving in to grief, my mother's daughter
picked up the yellow Lab's guide dog harness handle and
headed out to a bookstore café, where,
with the weight of a sleeping dog's head on her feet,
she wrote this poem in her head and held it in her heart.

A Daughter's Goodbye

> In memory of William Bennett, 1922–2000

Gaunt beyond his seventy-seven years,
my dying father sleeps, sedated,
beneath crisp white sheets and blankets
on a bed from which he will never rise.

Kidney cancer has invaded nearby organs
and claimed his bloodstream as its transport
around his skeletal body that lingers
on the brink of a new century.

Outside the icy hospice window,
dusk falls on the final day of a century
and tucks its comfort tenderly
around my father in his remaining hours.

No stranger to floating through the sky
with an army parachute down
to the chaos and carnage of Normandy's beaches,
he survived to lose this universal battle.

His imminent journey will, I hope,
be gentler and more peaceful
as his soul transcends time and ether
while, sadly, I release his hand.

Shadow

Seeking refuge from the relentless summer sun,
he arrived on my patio
unbidden and collarless.
His plaintive meows brought forth
bowls of food and water as
he watched, warily, from a distance.
He returned mornings and evenings
for meals and eventual friendship,
winding his ginger tabby bulk around my legs
and kneading his large white paws on my lap
as I stroked his scarred body.
When the chill of autumn tinged the breeze,
he made a decision, and with
his name tag swaying softly from
his new collar, he resolutely, and
without a backward glance, walked through
my front door into the security
of his forever home.

Farewell

My husband's aunt stands before me,
elderly and frail, mind wandering in dementia's fog.
The lunch we shared will be our last,
cake crumbs swept away like memories.
Only one of us knows
we will not meet again.
Wanting her closer, her children are
moving her time zones from here.
I hug her tightly and whisper, "I love you."
Patting my back, she replies in kind,
kisses me, and strokes my guide dog's head.
Smiling for her sake, I turn to leave
as my heart constricts with sadness.

My Hands

At sixty–two, life appears surprisingly finite,
and I think of the things my hands have never done,
such as hold a baby of my own, write Ph.D. after my name, and
holding a walking stick, traverse the rugged Welsh landscape.
I consider the things my hands have done,
such as wear the wedding rings of two difficult marriages,
shepherd both parents through hospice care, and
welcome five stray cats and two guide dogs into my home and
    heart.
I marvel at the things my hands might yet do
such as grasp the harness handle of my third guide dog,
write a novel, and pray for compassion,
because life is finite.

Letting Go and Holding On

When winter comes, I clean my home
and turn toward spring with a lighter load.
In old age, I need less
of living's daily clutter.
Cherished books sit on friends' shelves
or hide like gems at book sales.
The sofa and china will outlive me,
and I don't want the trendy coffeemaker my husband covets.
My size six jeans have gone to thrift stores
along with my hope of being so slender again.

What I long to keep slips away
at alarmingly breakneck speed.
My husband sinks deeper into depression and pain.
Two friends tell me of advanced cancers.
Dogs and cats I miss are ashes underground.
I thank God Laurence remains
to guide me through life's mazes.
I hold today, like a small bird,
in cupped hands and release her
with prayers for strength and patience.

The Gift

When my paratrooper father jumped out of an airplane sixty-nine years ago and landed on the Normandy beach during the D-Day invasion, he was only one of five men in his company who survived. Scarcely twenty-two and with a few years of war behind him, he returned to his base in England and married his English girlfriend after the whirlwind romance common in wartime. Within three years, the couple had moved to a small town in Pennsylvania to begin their married life without the separation and anxiety of war.

If my father had any of the post-traumatic stress disorder so common to today's returning troops, he never displayed it or spoke much about his war experiences. Instead, he chose to settle in his hometown among a close-knit family, raise two children, and enjoy the small pleasures of everyday life, since one never could take them for granted. Having survived the war, my father knew all too well that fate was random and life was to be cherished—especially when life took some unexpected turns, such as a daughter who began losing vision in middle age, and his doctor confirmed a diagnosis of kidney cancer shortly after my father retired.

Because my family did what loving families do, I offered my father a kidney, and he told me he wished he could give me his eyes. As it turned out, he was not able to receive a transplant and died two years before I became totally blind and applied for a guide dog from Guiding Eyes for the Blind. Although I was sorry to have lost my father as well as all of my light perception,

I was even sorrier that my father, a lifelong dog lover, would never meet my guide dog or know how much that dog enhanced my life.

When my first guide dog, Boise, arrived for home training in 2003, I was told that her Guiding Eyes identification tattoo was BB0001; this meant that she was born into the second litter of puppies all given names beginning with B in the year 2000 and that she was the first-born of her litter. That was certainly one way to understand her tattoo, but I realized there was another far more important way to interpret it: my father, Bill Bennett, who had died on January 1, 2000. BB0001. I am a woman who, over the years, has learned to look for and be grateful for signs and omens. As I stroked Boise's broad head, I smiled through tears and knew with absolute certainty that my father, safe from war and illness, had sent me a message through my dog's tattoo number. He might not have been able to give me his own eyes, but my father knew that another creature would provide the help his daughter needed.

Oxygen

Lying awake in the pre-dawn,
I listen to the steady whoosh
of my sleeping husband's respirator
and smooth rough stones of words
into the polished quartz of poetry.

Across the room, the dogs snore
and shift in their sleep.

Matching my breath to
the machine's steady rhythm, I filter
the carbon dioxide of worry from my body.

The pure air of creation fills me
and keeps me alive in the dark.

The Last Spring

We have grown old together, my guide dog and I.
Although, nearing ten, she is older in dog years
than I am at sixty-one. While my hair has long
been silver, her yellow fur has only
recently faded to the white of old age.

We have grown wise together, my guide dog and I.
We have stood steadfastly by the graves of loved ones and
have turned from the freshly dug mounds of earth,
leaving our pink and lavender bouquets behind.

We have grown frail together, my guide dog and I.
We welcome the warm spring sun on our aging bodies
and the soft breezes that follow us on this last part of our
    journey.

We will part as she retires, my guide dog and I.
She lies in a patch of sunlight, paws twitching
in pursuit of dream squirrels—living, as dogs do, in the moment.
Only I, in my human sadness
know this will be our last spring.

Each Day a Blessing

The jangle of her collar and
the click of toenails on the kitchen floor
flood me with relief in the pre–dawn.
Today will not be the day I wake my husband
with the news his service dog has died.
Nearly fourteen, she has survived another night,
Rising, albeit stiffly, despite the indignities of old age.

Her soft muzzle touches my hand expectantly
for the biscuit I offer each morning.
Following a crunch, her nose sniffs my hand again,
her tail thumping against a cabinet as
another treat slips into her eager mouth.
Two old ladies with their quiet ritual
of biscuits and coffee greet the dawn.

Her nose insistently bumps my arm for a third treat.
I give it, along with an admonishment of
"No more!" in mock severity, showing empty hands.

She licks my fingers in thanks or
in search of crumbs and pads down the hall
while, smiling, I reach for my mug.

Laurence's Promise

She wasn't prepared to love him so fiercely,
this somber black Labrador Retriever who arrived
to become her third and, perhaps, last guide dog.

He sized her up quickly with intelligent eyes,
this aging woman standing before him,
worn down by her burdensome sack of worries and sorrow,
and intuited she needed more than his guide work.

When she sat and called his name, he lovingly rested
his broad head on her lap and
made her understand he would bury that sack in a deep, deep
    hole
and care for her with all his gentle being.

Beyond Bereft

Laundry can wait;
my dog needs me as
he curls beside me and sighs
while I stroke his soft ears.

Email can wait;
my dog needs me as
he wanders our home searching
for my husband's retired service dog.

Phone calls can wait;
my dog needs me when,
lost without his canine friend,
he gnaws a bone, attempting consolation.

Dinner can wait;
my dog needs me when
he snatches his favorite toy from me
and tugs with wagging tail.

Everything can wait;
my dog and I need each other as
we step into the future with full hearts.

Loss

A week before my husband died,
I lost my wedding ring.
It slipped, unnoticed, from my finger
and rolled away forever
onto a coffee shop's parking lot,
among apples in the produce department,
or into wet grass at dusk.

I searched to no avail
and hoped it would magically appear
under our kitchen table,
beneath socks in the laundry basket,
or in the dryer's lint filter.

A week after I lost my wedding ring,
my husband died when a burst aneurysm
flooded his brain at breakfast.
Holding his hand in intensive care and
signing organ donation forms, I knew
my husband, like the ring, was gone forever.

Two Vigils

Vending machine coffee,
bitter and now lukewarm,
sits neglected in the stark light
of the intensive care unit's
time warp and uncertainty.

Family members, as one, crane necks
as swinging doors open and
strain to hear awaited news
from anyone passing in white.

Beyond tired, this small clutch of
relatives perch on unyielding plastic,
united in love and anxiety,
not unlike my family days before
in a waiting room far away.

This family, not mine, will end
its vigil in joy, grateful for
the gift of life my husband's liver
has bestowed upon someone they love.

Running Free

A not uncommon practice,
two souls amble along the water's edge,
leaving prints in cool wet sand
and relishing the time before them.

Warmed, not burned, by a rising sun,
these old friends enjoy the peace
found in one another's company
as seagulls shriek and dive.

Tossing driftwood high into salty air,
the man laughs as his dog takes chase.
Unencumbered by wheelchairs and service dog vests,
they race along eternity's shore.

Fragments of Poems

Fragments of poems lie
sleeping inside me,
not ready to face the light of day.

Too many losses and hardships,
one after another,
froze them in mid-verse.

A winter of bone-chilling cold,
illness and family deaths,
my husband's deepening depression—
these are poetry's fodder,
but not just now.

Words that could turn life's dross
into expressive, shimmering gold
elude me in this dry season.

Sipping my morning coffee while
stroking my dog's soft ears,
I find hope in the songs
of chirping birds outside my window
and believe that words, like spring,
will, despite a barren winter, come once more.

Hopeful Hands

Each day I wake
with hopeful hands
willing to perform
purposeful tasks
or kind, random acts.

The stupor of grief
has lifted and left me
bewildered on strange paths,
adrift at sea,
holding a broken compass
and with no stars to guide me.

While autumn turns to
winter, my hands busy
themselves of their own
accord while my spirit,
like hard ground, lies fallow,
waiting for the warmth of spring.

The Chosen

Knowing I need her, she will
come to take me home,
away from this place of steel and stress.

Others of my kind here
curl up tightly with eyes closed.
Some hiss and extend sharp claws,
fear hiding their true natures.

Feline angels from her past
whisper of her preparations
for my rescue and homecoming.
Catnip mice and jugs of litter
fill a corner of a room,
just as I will fill a space
carved into her heart by recent loss.

She knows cats choose their humans
and that I await her arrival.
My head resting against my cage,
I will see her when she comes,
and she will know me by
the loving, rumbling purrs
welling up from my soul's depth.

Silent Night

Edges of memories
from holidays past
blur into one another,
softening the sharpness
of longing and grief.

Perfection, illusory in hindsight,
like Christmas card scenes,
was never the reality.

The trappings of tinsel
and snow-covered fields
masked the true messages
of faith and family.

Much older now, I sit
and gratefully remember
a cup of ginger tea
and a contented cat's purrs
as company on this tranquil night.

Sitting in the Dark

Sitting in the dark at four in the morning
with an audiobook to fill the empty hours,
I think of my no-nonsense British mother
who faced old age and grief head-on with cups of milky tea
and the printed company of Rosamunde Pilcher and P. D. James
to link her to the long-ago past of parents, greengrocers, and village halls.

Victory gardens, ration books, and nights spent in air-raid shelters
taught her early that life was fragile and unfair but
still worth living with fortitude, humor, and faith.
Picking up the invisible thread that binds generations to one another,
I put the kettle on and continue reading as dawn approaches.

Living with Intention

Living with intention
seems beyond my grasp
as my insistent alarm clock
jolts me from troubling dreams,
propelling me into another day
of Covid lockdown and isolation.

My hungry cat's mews remind me
to flex arthritic joints
and squarely face the day.

Here

Eleven months have come and gone
since I became a widow.
One moment rearranged my world
in ways I'd yet to fathom.

I thought perhaps he would be near,
a partner on my journey.
In a silent home, I strained to catch
his voice or find proof his spirit lingered.

No intuition or wondering prayer
brought forth a true connection
until isolation slowed my pace,
and I had time to listen.

I felt his presence like
a cloak of caring and protection
that warmed my body and frozen soul
and offered hope of resurrection.

Liminal Time

When my husband died two years ago, I believed his death would be a dividing line in my life. "Before" was the time we shared, and "After" began as I kissed him for the last time and left his body in a hospital room, taking up my metaphorical widow's weeds.

What I had no way of knowing was that I was about to enter liminal time, the threshold between "before" and "after." I could not go back in time and did not see a path forward alone. While I was certainly sad and grieved, I was stuck, in limbo, caught on the threshold to God knew what.

As the raw shock of loss lessened and I was left with occasional waves of sorrow, I expected to pack away my widow's weeds and rejoin the world beyond my grief. I reasoned that the rest of my life was mine for the taking, filled with new adventures and old friends.

Were it not for a pandemic arriving within less than a year of my husband's passing, I might have become the woman, two years shy of seventy, who finally traversed the rugged Welsh terrain, joined a local women's choir, and enjoyed her morning coffee while dough for home-baked multigrain bread rose on her stove. However, I am none of those women. Wales remains a dream, I sing silly songs to my tolerant cat, and my bread comes from a grocery store.

For the first year of the pandemic, I consoled myself with the knowledge that everyone's lives were on hold. Now, as the threat of death and illness from a raging virus lessens, I am still perched on the threshold, wondering when liminal time slips quietly into "after" and if I will notice that I have missed the opportunity to step into a future of my choosing.

Night Visitor

She came to me in a deep sleep's dream
or perhaps in the moment hovering between dawn and waking.
Although we had not met, I felt no fear
as I knelt before her sitting bulk.

Her soft, warm muzzle nudged my hand,
and I cupped it before my fingers moved up to silky ears
and the thick ruff that almost hid her collar.
Tracing solid shoulders and a strong back,
I felt my eager fingers move to grasp
a harness handle, but hesitated
because this canine visitor did not belong to me.

In wordless communion, we spoke heart language
as she told me she was waiting for me on the pandemic's other
        side,
to walk beside me and guide me through my seventies.
Cautioning her that my older body and quiet days
might mean I could not meet her there,
I knew we would be together in other lives and forms,
because love transcends time and place.

As she faded into the night or dawn,
I woke to feel the lingering warmth of her fur on my hands
and a flickering light in my soul.

Nine Months

Nine months ago today,
my husband died on
an unseasonably cold
and bleak May morning.

Unrelenting rain pelted
windows at the end
of the hospital hallway
as his family and I,
having left his body behind,
waited for a down elevator.

One of his sisters, who
had spoken little to me
in years, uncharacteristically
called me an amazing woman
as we huddled under
a useless umbrella on
our way to a waiting car.

She was mistaken.
I was in shock and
thought the weather
mirrored my loss.

Nine months later, it is
a warm February day,

Peonies in Winter

with rain rather than snow.
Be it climate change or
Nature's bewilderment at
the death of one good man
and at my life still
turned upside down,
the elemental gods
offer small comfort.

Night Wind

Insistent wind rattles the windows,
jarring me from healing sleep.
It howls through bare branches and
bends them into submission or,
because it can, snaps the defiant.
Morning will be time enough
to ascertain damage.

I have reached an age when
resilience against life's storms and pain
is better measured in the light of day.
Tucking my blankets close
around my aching body, I sigh
and slip back into the welcome unknowing.

Brittle with Age

Brittle with age, the British aerogram's
corner crumbles in my hand.
One of many letters lovingly saved
in a granddaughter's once–pink hair ribbon
for more than six decades, it is
a bittersweet attempt to bear witness
and turn thin sheets of paper
into crinkled forget–me–nots.

As a child, I believed
aerograms were blue to match
the ocean they traversed
from an elderly lady in Leicestershire
to a schoolgirl in Pennsylvania.

I know the spidery handwriting
relates only family news
and inquires about my school days,
Brownie troop, and beloved dogs.
Missives of love from one brittle with age,
of no interest to intrusive eyes after my death,
the aerograms and bond they forged
can remain tucked away for now.

The ink has no doubt faded over time,
but the memories in the heart of the granddaughter,
herself now brittle with age,
remain fresh with just a hint of ocean breeze.

Tamsin in Repose

Startled awake in the early hours,
still held in a distant nightmare's grasp,
I try to follow the dream's thread,
hoping to unravel horror's hold
enough to sleep without fear.
Beside me, Tamsin stirs, sensing my unease.
Stroking her warm, soft, feline fur,
I marvel at her ability
to accept the sanctuary of this room
and wonder if she is ever haunted
by past terrors of her feral life.
Snuggling closer, she lets me know
that memories, like dreams in the dark,
fade into the present light of love.

A Matter of Perspective

Clutching the nickel Grandpa had just given me, I stood in front of the penny candy counter and made my usual choices from the selection of chocolate, licorice, taffy, and hard candy on display behind the glass. A lover of all things chocolate, my first choice was always the small chocolate square called "Gray Day."

I was a pragmatic child who knew a good deal when she saw it. Gray Days were two for a penny. The only drawback about them was that I thought, given their name, they could only be purchased on cloudy days. I considered the chocolate squares a special treat, one meant to make rainy cloudy days better.

When I learned to read, I was confused to see the term "Grade A" etched onto them. Premium penny candy, not one to dispel gloomy weather.

Still, I reasoned, the candy tasted the same no matter what it was called, and the price was certainly a good one. However, there was still a small part of my four-year-old self that missed the imaginary potion of them. I missed the special power of a chocolate "Gray Day."

While I am no longer that child, I have carried what I call "the Gray Day lesson" with me throughout the years. It has served me well, but never so much as in the months following Sandy's death and the time spent in my apartment during the pandemic.

Two and a half years since my husband died, I wake most mornings believing he is still sleeping beside me. A nice memory, but not the best way to greet a new day. I remind myself that each day has the same number of hours and that, despite the disappointment of realizing I am alone, I can choose how I fill those hours. Now that I am no longer Sandy's caregiver, the hours before me can drag with no structure or expand to be filled with tasks of my own choosing.

Choosing freedom of choice, I plan my days. After feeding my cat, Tamsin, and sitting down with a cup of coffee, I spend as much time as needed in prayer, meditation, and naming gratitudes. Centering myself lightens me and allows me to see the day ahead as one full of possibilities rather than lingering sorrow.

I must admit that, catless as I then was, I didn't start the days following Sandy's death in the above manner. Pouring a mug of coffee and listening to music was the most I could manage. For months after Sandy died, I started my days listening to the same two songs on my smart speaker: "Nothing Is Wasted," by contemporary Christian singer Jason Gray, and "The Point of Arrival," by Quaker singer-songwriter Carrie Newcomer. Over and over. Something in the music found its way through grief's numbness. As the months progressed, my frozen heart thawed bit by bit until I was able to incorporate Gray's and Newcomer's lessons into my life.

Life is far from perfect, so not every morning begins with prayer and purpose. Holidays are especially difficult, and there are still days when grief appears suddenly out of nowhere and punches me in the gut. At times such as these, I make tea, hug Tamsin close, and lose myself in a new Ann Cleeves or Louise Penny novel...and oh yes, a little chocolate never hurts.

Resources

What sort of former librarian and occupational therapist would I be if I failed to leave readers with no ideas for continued growth? The small selection of books below is purposely short. Grief often makes decision-making difficult; a long bibliography could be overwhelming. Because it is important to me that readers can easily locate titles, these books are all recent publications. More important to me, as someone who is blind, is that all these resources can be found in numerous audio editions as well as in print. Given the ease of searching for all types of formats online, I have noted only the title and author and omitted the bibliographic information for print versions.

Nonfiction

Kate Mosse
An Extra Pair of Hands

Rachel Clarke
Dear Life: A Doctor's Story of Love and Loss

David Kessler
Finding Meaning: The Sixth Stage of Grief

Lucy Hone
Resilient Grieving: Finding Strength and Embracing Life After a Loss that Changes Everything

Jacqueline Winspear

This Time Next Year We'll Be Laughing

Fiction

Alison Ragsdale
Finding Heather

Abbi Waxman
The Garden of Small Beginnings

Dani Atkins
Gone Too Soon

Acknowledgments

I would like to thank the following people and organizations for their support and encouragement:

Pastor Karyn Wiseman and the members of Gloria Dei Lutheran Church in Huntingdon Valley, Pennsylvania

Guiding Eyes for the Blind in Yorktown Heights, New York—in particular the Specialized Training Program

Elissa, Kelli, and the rest of the editorial staff of Best Friends Animal Society in Kanab, Utah

Online friends from the GEB Grads list, the Blind Faith group, and all the Doves

A heartfelt "shout out" to librarians everywhere and the angels working in animal rescue

Colleagues from online writers' groups, especially Behind Our Eyes and Writers' Retreat: Abbie, Alice, Annie, Bonnie, Carol, Cleora, DeAnna, Deborah, James, Kate, Leonard, Marcia, Marilyn, Marlene, Mary Jo, Valerie, Winslow, and many other talented authors with disabilities

Individuals who enrich my life through their presence: Andrea, Anita, Betsy and Rich, Bill and Rose, Diane, Donna, Evelyn, Joanne, Judy and Skip, Kate, Kim, Lynda and Jeff, Mary, Melissa, Rita, Sandy, Sharon, Sian, and Susan

If I have neglected to mention people whose names should have been included above, I am mortified by my negligence but still treasure our connection.

Anyone who knows me personally or through my work must realize the importance of animals throughout my family history and lifetime. Not to acknowledge the dogs and cats who have inspired and loved me would be a huge oversight. In addition to my three guide dogs, Boise, Greta, and Laurence, and Sandy's service dog, Pumpkin, the following dogs have graced my life: Peter Palmer, Kim Palmer, Kip Turnbull, Boots Bennett, Toby Hipple, Corky Bennett, Wimpy Hartman, Sam Brandt, Keeny Bennett, Sandy Bennett, Charlie Bennett, Charcoal Bennett, Maggie Bennett, Kate Bennett, and Scooter Bennett. The following cats have chosen me: Hocus Rosenthal, Pocus Rosenthal, Ziggy Rosenthal, Shadow Rosenthal, Toby Rosenthal, and, of course, Tamsin Bennett–Rosenthal.

About the Author

Born prematurely in 1952, Sally Rosenthal survived a stroke in infancy and lost her vision slowly from complications of retinopathy of prematurity. She is also, without hearing aids, profoundly deaf due to age-related genetic hearing loss. A former academic librarian and occupational therapist, she now writes for a variety of online and print publications. A vegetarian and staunch animal rights advocate, she lives with her cat, Tamsin, in a large East Coast American city but dreams of waking one morning in a cottage on the north coast of Cornwall.

Contact Information

Website: https://www.dldbooks.com/sallyrosenthal/

Email: sanford.rosenthal@comcast.net